The **A**id of the Shepherd

Choose among you seven men full of the
Holy Ghost, honest, of good report...

by Dr. Gerald Thomas, Sr.

The Aid of

the

Shepherd

© Copyright, 2014

by

Gerald Thomas, Sr.

ISBN – 978-0-9852206-5-5
Library of congress number: 2014939277

Cover designed by Water for The Journey, Inc.

Photography

Editors:

DGPUBLISHING, INC.
2720 Blair Stone Rd.
Tallahassee, FL 32304
www.dgpublishingpress.com
850-566-8169

Preface

This book will help assist pastors across denominational barriers equip their deacons to see the warfare in the office of an untrained deacon. Also, the book provides a textbook model for workshops and leadership training. What is more, this book administers to pastors, deacons and lay leaders in the church that need to know what this office consist of. To some degree, it informs the church how to reach its full potential with the office of deacon. This book shows the ministry strategy of two scriptural offices working hand in hand. You may use this book as a guide to format suitable structures for newly organized churches. With biblical outlines from this manuscript, you can make modification and adjustments to accommodate your ministry. The intention of this book is that it aids you in establishing order in the church as it relates to the office of pastor and deacon.

Dedication

To my wife Marilyn D. Thomas, my daughters Aesha V. Thomas, Geralyn L. Thomas, son Gerald Thomas Jr. and New Direction Christian Center of Quincy, Florida.

We can reach the least, lost and the last together!

CONTENTS

Introduction

Arise, shine; for thy light is come, and the glory of the Lord is risen upon thee. For, behold, the darkness shall cover the earth, and gross darkness the PEOPLE: BUT THE Lord shall rise upon thee, and his glory shall be seen upon thee, and the Gentiles shall come to thy light, and kings to the brightness of thy rising. Isaiah 60:1-3. These verses tell of a time of grace, and great spiritual influence. Isaiah saw the impact of the coming of Jesus Christ. He saw the great light that would come into the world during the advent of the Savior.

The age of grace is an age of truth. Abraham saw the coming of the day of Christ, and it made him glad. (St. John8:56) The coming of the spiritual light would bring joy to the world, such as when darkness flees at the rising of the sun. Jesus is the day spring. He is the source of the light. In the light of divine truth there is salvation. Remember how the Lord said, "Ye shall know the truth and the truth shall make you free." (St. John 8:32). The day of Jesus Christ is here. The day of grace, and truth, has come to this world of darkness, and sin. Remember, how John said," for the law was give by Moses, but the grace and truth came from Jesus Christ (St. John 1:17). Yes, Jesus is truth and light. (St. John 14:6, 9:5) We are children of the day and we must walk in the light of the Son of God. In the modern Christian church, God calls his people to the light. Truth is light and truth makes us free. Those persons who are deacons and those who are in training for deaconship should realize that we have a challenge from heaven itself to arise and walk in the light of the Son of God. Then shall we be able to serve and magnify the Lord. There is power in truth, both to save and deliver. Jesus Christ is our light; let us arise to walk with him. "This is the message which we have heard of him and declare unto you that God is light and in him there is no darkness at all.

If we say that we have fellowship with him and walk in darkness, we lie, and we have fellowship one with another and the blood of Jesus Christ his Son cleanseth us from all sin. (1 John 1:5-7) As we study the Deacon on Duty, we will stand in the light of God's truth. Let us arise to this challenge of learning. Light concerning the deacon and his work is risen upon you. Standing in the light of God's truth, let us go forward to do God's will. Remembering, "For they that have used the

2

office of a deacon well purchase to themselves a good degree and great boldness in the faith which is in Jesus Christ (see 1 Timothy 3:13.)

Deacon Motto

I will take the work of the deaconship seriously. the aid of the pastor, the advancement of the gospel, and the peace of the church my aim; Looking unto Jesus, the author, and finisher of our faith.

THE DEACON'S MEETING

When the time for the deacon's meeting has come, strive to be on time. Being prompt for meeting is good. When you are on time the pastor, and/or other brothers, do not have to delay the business at hand. Don't be the one everybody is waiting on. Be sure that all the brothers know the date, time, and place of the meeting. The meeting times will be set by the pastor in conference with the staff members. No meeting of deacons should take place without pastor's presence or approval. There will be times when the pastor will not be able to meet with the deacons. However, the pastor, usually in conference will prescribe the agenda with all chairmen of the deacon staff. The pastor will preside at all meetings the exception to this rule is in the absence other pastor, or chairman. The presiding officer must at all times confer with the pastor on all agenda items.

Deacon meetings should never cover making, or establishing the duty roster. Deacon meetings should be training and study times. Deacon meetings are times when the pastor can share his vision with the brothers. The deacon's meeting is a time of fellowship with pastor and staff. Be a good listener. Help of the work. Strive to be cooperative with the other deacons. Remember team work, works. Read and study Psalm 133, this number embraces brotherhood committed to advancing the gospel of Jesus Christ through their assistance to the man of God.

Check with the pastor from time to time. See if there are any special or current needs that the brothers may not be aware. Pray for the other brothers. Pray for the pastor something to remember. As a general rule, let the meeting be brief. You cannot accomplish everything in one meeting. If the meeting are brief and to the point, the brothers and pastor will look forward to the gathering rather than dread it. Sometimes just come together briefly to pray and share experiences. Be a brother to the brothers. Remember you are imperfect too. Be a man of peace with love for one another. Say the deacon motto and follow the agenda for the day. Keep the

Bible purpose for the deacon always before you. Adjourn with a prayer.

1

Deaconship

Definition, Distinction and Qualification.

When we speak of the deaconship or talking about the work of a deacon, its nature and scope, in the church of today, there are many varied views. As it relates to the nature and scope of the work of the deacon in too many churches today, there are faulty concepts of deaconship. These concepts are the source of confusion and strife. Evil operates best in darkness. Darkness is Satan's workshop. In Satan's workshop he forges the instruments of destruction.

Whenever God's people labor without the benefit of Divine light, Satan wreaks havoc in the midst. Satan can take one ignorant man and destroy years of good work. "Wisdom is better than weapons of war: but one sinner destroyeth much good."(Ecclesiastes 9:18) One Sinner can destroy so much good because he is blind to the worth and beauty of good. The destroying element in the sinner is ignorance whether it resides with unbelievers.

Blindness is an instrument of destruction. The all-wise God looked on his people's condition in the days of the prophet and saw Satan destroying many with the sword rejected knowledge, I will also reject thee, that thou shalt be not priest to me: seeing thou has forgotten the law of thy god, I will also forget thy children." (Hosea 4:6) If you will notice this verse in Hosea you will discover that darkness which is the lack of knowledge was destroying contagion among the people, but he source of the problem was the priest. The priest had then the same responsibility toward the people as pastors have now. Remember, how it is written of Levi the father of priest. "And shall know that I have sent this commandment unto you, that my covenant might be with Levi, saith the Lord of hosts.

My covenant was with him of life and peace; and I gave them to him for the fear wherewith he feared me, and was afraid before my name. The law of truth was in his mouth and iniquity was not found in his lips; he walked with me in peace and equity and did turn many away from iniquity. For the priest's lips should keep knowledge and they should seek the law at his mouth: for he is the messenger of the Lord of hosts. (Malachi 2:4-7) Jesus charges his shepherds as he charged Simon Peter saying, feed my sheep; feed my lambs" (John 21:15-17.) Also he commanded the preacher to teach his people. "Teaching them to observe all things whatsoever I commanded you; and, lo I am with you always even unto the end of the world." Amen. (Matthew 28:20) When as in the time of the prophet Hosea the priest or pastors failed or ceased to be disciples of truth, they also failed or ceased to be disciples of truth, they also failed and ceased to be teachers of truth. Destruction with darkness enveloped the people because these charged with their instruction took their work too lightly. Destruction came to the people had rejected knowledge. Because thou hast rejected knowledge, I will also reject thee that thou shalt be no priest to me; seeing thou hast forgotten the law of God." The office of the deacon was created to aid the Gospel ministers to pursue the study of the word. Remember, the verse mentioned in the introduction of this book. "To whom we may appoint over this business? But we will give ourselves continually to prayer and to the ministry of the word." (Act 6:3-4) The Lord's shepherds should be specialists in the word, bringing to then people the great light of truth. Thus in this study we endeavor to dismiss the darkness of ignorance and the destruction which accompany it. Let us therefore with diligence, study the word. The Deacons service will help to give pastors this crucial time so necessary to enlighten the people.

The Word Deacon, its Meaning and Application

Our word deacon is derived from the Greek word, Siakovos (diakonos) it means one who serves, a servant employed in some capacity; however, its special scripture application is to the second class of church offices. There are two scriptures officers min the church, one is pastor and the second is deacon.

The earliest record of deacons in the New

Definition Distinction and Qualification.

Testament church is found in the sixth chapters of Acts. Though church is found in the sixth chapter of Acts, the work of the deacon is found there. The title of this office holder came after the events of (Act 6.) Those men who served tables were by their work denoted as deacons. Hence, later in scripture when referred to them as siakavos, these men served tables in the church) So, that in Acts chapter six you have the work described and the personal names of men then chosen. In Philippians 1:1, you have the word, "deacon" which later became the accepted name or title of them who served the tables of the church. We also find the reference to deacons in 1Timothy 3:8. By the time of the writing of Philippians and Timothy the name of the office of those who served tables was well established in the churches.

The Distinction of the Deaconship

Now, please let us note the distinction between the office of the preacher and/or pastor in the church from that of the deacon. The deacon and the preacher have servant officers in the church; however, the distinction comes in two areas:

1. The work of the deacon is temporal, the servicing of tables. Please note the scripture. "Then the twelve called the multitude of the disciples unto them and said it is not reason that we should leave the word of God and serve tables.

2. Wherefore, brethren, look ye out among you seven men of honest report, full of the Holy Ghost and wisdom, which we may appoint over this business." (Act 6:2-3)

We will farther examine and explore these passengers more thoroughly as well as others, but for now let us be clear as to the fact that the deaconship is distinct from that of the gospel preacher. The work of the deacon therefore is the physical serving of the tables in the church. The deaconship, (the office of the deacon) is primarily temporal of physical in natural things.

3. In contrast the primary work of the preacher is spiritual. The gospel ministry is laboring in the word of God. The minister of the gospel must be able to focus on the word of God. The word is spiritual. The ministers of the gospel have as their charge

4. the keys of the kingdom of heaven. Keys are representative of the power to open and shut. In the gospel there is power to deliver and there is power to discipline. It was to Peter (who was representative of those with the preaching and pastoral charge) that our Lord said, "And I will give unto thee the keys of the kingdom of heaven: and whatsoever thou shalt bind on earth shall be bound in heaven.

5. And whatsoever thou shalt loose on earth shall be loosed in heaven." (Matthew 16:19) Remember, brother deacons and those of you who are training for the deaconship your office was created by the ministers of the gospel for the purpose of freeing the gospel ministers from having to distribute material goods to needy members of the church. Serving the tables was and is the task of the deacons. We understand therefore the work of the deacon differs and is distinct from that of the gospel ministers both in (1) the nature of their

work (one is primarily temporal dealing with physical goods and the other is

6. spiritual dealing primarily with the preaching of the word and it's preparation). The office of the deacon and the office of the preacher are distinct not only in the nature of the work. (2) They are distinctive in purpose. The purpose of the deacons is to aid the gospel preacher by faithfully and justly serving the tables of the church. There are three tables in the New Testament church: The tables represent areas of responsibility and obligation of the church to provide support. Men should quality for the work of receiving these offerings.

The Deaconship: The Qualifications

The apostles faced with responsibilities of a growing church found that there was a need for another class of officers. There was a need for another class of officers. There was a need for godly men who unlike themselves did not have the responsibility of preaching the Word of God. God had called the apostles to take the gospel to the world. There was such a gathering of souls that the day to day needs of benevolence for many of these people loaded the apostles with work, details that threatened to take them away from their primary work. " Then the twelve called the multitude of the disciples unto them, and said, it is not reason that we should leave the work of God and serve tables (Acts 6:2)."

The apostles must preach and teach that word which is the power of God unto salvation. They must not leave the word of God to serve tables. Yet the tables need serving. There were many needs. Someone must do this work. Someone must serve the tables. Many in the church were poor and needed assistance from the body of believers. The church had accepted the responsibility to minister to spiritual and physical need of its members; hence, the need for deacons.

It was the need of the widows in the Church that made the call up of these officers necessary "and in those days when the number of the disciples was multiplied, there arose a murmuring of the Grecians against the Hebrews because their widows were neglected in the daily ministration". (Acts 6:1) to serve the tables' the apostles needed men to whom they could assign to this work. They would need men with three special character credits. They needed men who were known for their (1) Honesty, (2) Full of the Holy Ghost, (3) wisdom. The nature of the deacon's work required honesty, a spirit-filled life, and wisdom.

Without men meeting these requirements they will become an apostles, there was honesty, Spirit filled lives and wisdom, but their problem of murmuring members had arisen because the workload was too great. They had little time after study and prayer to reach, and meet the needs of all widows who had applied for aid. Many of the members were already murmuring, so it would not be wisdom to assign just anyone to this work. The deacons must have character equipment alone with moral and spiritual credibility.

Honest Deacons

The deacon should be an honest man. Honest is a requirement because the deacons stand at the offering table to receive the gifts of the people. Not to be honest is to be a thief. The church does not need thieves at its offering tables. Care must be taken to choose men who have a honest report. If you don't know anything about him, he is not ready for deaconship. Let us be sure that those who are selected to be deacons in the church "have" an honest report. It is not wisdom to accept one's word that the man under consideration has an honest report.

The man chosen to be a deacon should have a record of honest dealings. When we look closely at the qualifications of a deacon we see why there has been so much trouble and problems at the tables. Thieves and dishonesty will plague the church and pastor who take too lightly the men who occupy the deaconship. The twelve had had firsthand experience with a thief carrying the bag. Remember what the scripture said about the treasure of Jesus' little church. The wicked treasurer complained that instead of using costly ointment to anoint the minister who in this case was Jesus. He argued a better use could have been made of those funds. Notice what he said and what could have been made of those funds. Look at what he said and what the scripture said about him. Judas said, "Why was not this ointment sold for three hundred pence and given to the poor?

(John 12:5) Like Judas, dishonest men talk good, but doing good is never their intention. Dishonest people are not only thieves, but they also are liars. Notice, how the scripture evaluates Judas' speech, "This he said, not that he cared for the poor; but because he was a thief and had the bag, and bear what was put therein. (John 12:6) Hence, the apostles knew the danger and results of having a dishonest man at the offering tables of the church.

I am sure that Jesus chooses Judas as an object lesson for the church. He had other reasons also to choose a devil to be one of the twelve, but he also knew we would work with imitation disciples. So he choose one, that we might know that not all people in the church are the church. He wanted his church to know that Satan heads for the purse of the Church. Satan tries to put men at the tables of the church. The ministers and people must prayerfully consider who it is that stands there. Hence, the charge to the church, 'Wherefore, brethren, look ye out among you seven men of honest report, full of the Holy Ghost and wisdom." (Acts 6:3) Too many Christian bodies have read these words but failed to heed the warning and to earnestly carry out this charge. When we put a foe in the hen house why are we amazed when the chickens disappear? Honestly will bless the church as it ministers to the needs of its members. Honestly will cultivate good feelings and trust in the fellowship. Honesty will distribute the gifts with equity and fairness. Equity and fairness in action at the tables of the church will encourage continuous an increased giving, hence, expanding the capability of the church to meet more needs. Honesty will bless the work and ministry of the word because the pastor will have on fewer burdens, one less problem. Finally, the honest deacon will cast glory and honor upon the Lord who saved him.

He who bless the Lord; the Lord will bless. Serving faithfully, truthfully, and equitably will bring to pass the Lord's word spoken by Paul. "for they that have used the office of the a deacon well purchase to themselves a good degree and 2Timothy 3:13 seeing the need for honesty in them that stand at the tables of the church; we must ask for light from above in our choice of men for the deaconship.

Deacons Filled with the Holy Spirit

Once of the reasons why the deacon needs to be filled with the Spirit is a deacon needs to be motivated man. Spirit filled men do not burn out in the work. A Spirit filled deacon can understand the spiritual work of the man of God. He can see the relationship, as well as the distinction between his work and the work of the preacher. Spirit filled deacons understand that the pastor is a man of faith and the church is often called upon to move not by what may been seen, but rather by that which is hoped for. Men who know little or nothing about the Holy Spirit's impact on a surrendered life will be more of a burden, then help. The deacon especially is set apart to help the pastor to carry the burden of feeding the church. Deacons need to be Spirit filled men not only for understanding the pastor's task, but filling their task. The Holy Spirit is spiritual gasoline for the service. The Holy Spirit is power for burden bearing. The Holy Spirit is strength for "being and seeing" you cannot serve the tables if you are not at the tables. You must be in attendance regularly to be profitable in the stewardship of the deaconship "being" there is fifty percent of the job. We often have men who have good qualifications, but no matter how qualified you are if you cannot or will not be there when you are needed, then what good are all your qualifications. What good is a doctor, who is unavailable when the time comes to operate on the patient in need of surgery? What good is money when your bags are filled, your money is in a distant value and you stand with empty pockets in the check outline? What good is a praying deacon when he makes a habit out of missing prayer meeting and the devotional hour in worship? The Spirit filled deacon will have motivation from within to "be there" where and when he is needed.

The being full of the Holy Spirit will equip the deacon for seeing. You can physically "be" in a place and yet not function at the fullest capacity of if you are having trouble seeing. The Spirit filled deacon can see where and how he can serve best. He can see his assignment and ways to best accomplish it. Some people see everything, but cannot see anything they do wrong. They see what you are doing and what you need to do, but the right thing. Some see through just human eyes. They can see what you did wrong, but can't see anything they do wrong. They see what you are doing and what you need to do, but at that same time fail to see their own faults. The Holy Spirit will help you to see rightly. Remember, Jesus talked about that person who could see little more speck of dust in his brother's eyes, but was too blind to see a log his own.

As Jesus commanded, let us clear the problems of our shortcomings first rather than others. The Holy Spirit operating actively in our lives will show us where and how we can improve. The Spirit present us with help to be good "self-examiners" and by doing so will prevent the need for others to correct us. The Holy Spirit will help us with seeing situations and making sound decisions.

The Holy Spirit will not only equip the deacon for his service, but He will empower the deacon in his service. No life can be filled with the Spirit full of prayer. The Spirit filled deacon has learned and knows the power and the worth of prayer. He knows that ever so wise he cannot go against the powers of darkness on his own strength and knowledge alone. Whatever you bring to the equation of the answer, the Holy Spirit will be necessary to balance the equation. He (the Holy Spirit) knows the missing piece of any puzzle.

The Deacon and Wisdom

Wisdom must not be just something the deacon hears about. He must employ it in his own life and in his work in the church. Let us break down what wisdom is and how to use wisdom. A wise man is not just a man who possesses great knowledge. A man with wisdom not only knows facts, but knows how, where, and especially when to use the facts. Wisdom is the ability to use facts. Wisdom is the ability to see the relation between things. A knowledgeable soldier maybe an expert in the use and firing of any given weapon, but wisdom when to fire the weapon in any given situation or at all is the difference. A wise deacon knows where and when to apply his knowledge. Hence, the knowledgeable deacon must strive for wisdom. He must need to be a thinker and a learner. Wisdom requires thought and thought requires information. Deacons therefore must inform themselves especially about things required of him.

Deacons must know their work and he cannot know his work without communication with his pastor. The assignments are given by the pastor or by the chairman of the deacons who receive the assignments from the pastor. Yes, there are technical things that deacons perform, like devotion before worship service and receiving offering in service. Yet even for those things, communication with the pastor is crucial because the needs may vary from day to day or time to time. It is wisdom to know the work generally and to know your assignment. Individual deacons are often given individual tasks. Those individual tasks help accomplish the overall purpose of the work. Not only must the deacon be a student of his work, but he must be a student of the word. All believers, all Christian workers need a word. The Word of God is food for us. If the word be active and alive in our lives we shall be good witnesses of the saving power and grace of God. We must study to be wise. Living and serving with wisdom should be aim of the deacon.

The Deacon Working out of the Pastor's Office

Deacons get their assignments from the pastor. Let us now examine the deaconship "the text and the task," *"And in those days when the number of the disciples was multiplied, there arose a murmuring of the Grecians against the Hebrews because their widows were neglected in the daily ministration." (Acts 6:1)*

When we examine verse one we find (1) from whence came the need for deacons. The word of God had been preached and at that time being preached with power and conviction. The

23

Definition Distinction and Qualification.

Holy Spirit laboring through the office of the gospel ministry added many roles of the church. As it is written concerning those times. "And the Lord added to the church daily such as should be saved." (Acts 2:47) Hence, the phenomenal growth of the church created certain needs. This increased the work load of the apostles. There apostle not only had authority to declare the good grace of the kingdom, but only had authority to declare the good grace of the kingdom.

They also had charge of the gracious gifts offered by the church. (Acts 4:34-35, 37) Neither was there any among them that lacked: for as many as were possessors of lands or houses sold them, and then down at the apostles feet: distribution was made unto every man according as he had distribution was made unto every man according as he had need. Joses who by the apostle was surnamed Barnabas, (which is being interpreted, the son of consolation) a Levite and of the country of Cyrus having land, sold it and brought the money, and laid it at the apostle's feet. In addition to the charge of preaching the gospel, caring for the congregation the charge of the church treasury, and properties also were the responsibilities of the man with the kingdom keys. Because of the ministers authority in the church he could and did call the church together to consider a new proposal. The call from the preachers went out to the church. Yes, the whole church, men and women the multitude of the disciples unto them... (Saying) wherefore brethren look ye out among you because the action about to be taken would affect the whole church, so that there was a general gathering of the church. They did this to inform the body of believers concerning the selection of a new class of church officers. The church having gathered a specific call went out from the apostle to the men of the church. "Brethren look ye out from the apostle to the men of the church. Brethren check among the male members of the congregation.

The purpose of this search is that seven quality men to be chosen, men of honest report full of the Holy Ghost and wisdom that we may appoint over this business." (Acts 6:3).The specific call comes to the brethren. The order is for "seven men." When we discuss 1Timothy 3:8-11, we will discover the reason men are called up for the deaconship. Deacons are spiritual men during temporal task. Please understand while the deacon is distinct from the preacher/ pastor because of the distinct nature and purpose of his work; he is not independent of the pastor. Scripturally the deacon cannot say, "Pastor you do your work and I'll do my work." In reality the deacon works out of the office of the pastor. They work out of his office for three reasons:

1. The call for the deacons came from the preachers or pastors.
2. The call of assignments of the deacon is for the work that is responsibility of the minister.
3. The deacon is appointed to his work or assigned by the pastor. Hence, the deacon must report to the pastor.

Preaching the gospel, (Mark 3:14, Matthew 16:19; 28:19-20) administering the properties and charities of the church (Mark 16:19; Acts 4:34, 35, 37; 5:1-11) and caring for the membership all of these are pastoral responsibility, but with the selection of deacons all these particularly the serving of tables, "it is not reason" as a duty of the pastor. Yet, he cannot delegate the responsibility.

The deacon can and should perform the duty of serving the tables, but the responsibility for that duty belongs to the pastor. The charge of feeding the sheep is his alone. Jesus said to Peter, "Feed my sheep." Feed my Lambs. (see John 21:15-17; Acts 20:28; and also 1 Peter 5:1-2) The minister or the pastor has the oversight of the whole flock or congregation. Hence, the deacon works out of his office and under his leadership. Deacons therefore report to the pastor after having been appointed by the pastor to their particular task. Please notice that the church had nothing for the deacons to do. Had there been a job for the deacons to do then the call for deacons and to deacons would have come from the church. The call for the deacon and to the deacon came from preachers; the kingdom key men and it is to these men that the deacons report. The deacons are appointed over a particular business by the minister. Note the apostle words, "Wherefore brethren, look ye out among seven men whom we may appoint over this business." (Act 6:3) The appointing is seen in verse two, "then the twelve called the multitude." Now we come to the third reason that deacons work out of the office of the pastor. The pastor has the power of appointment. If the deacon is called up for service in an area of direct pastoral responsibility it is only reasonable that the pastor should appoint him to his work and receive reports of the same. Those who serve the table for which the pastor is responsible must report to him if they want to fulfill the purpose for which they are set aside. Remember, Brother Deacon, the appointer is in charge of and responsible for the work of the deaconship appointee.

A supervisor on a secular job does not have day to day duties of the people he is overseeing yet; he is responsible for the output or lack of output of those who work under his charge. Hence, the writer to the Hebrew Christian underscores pastoral accountability, which grows out of his responsibility for the conduct of the church membership. "Remember them when you have spoken unto the word of God: whose faith follows, considering the end of their conversation." (Hebrews 13:7) The above mentioned scriptures along with a few others that you will discover will help your study. Deacons should come to their work with good understanding and humility.

The deacon's wisdom should teach him the wisdom humility. God dwells with the humble. Wherever God is there is power and wherever God is there is peace. If the scriptures are very clear about the definition of the deaconship one may ask, why there is such confusion, conflict, and turmoil in the church it today relevant to the place and authority of deacons. The reason is found in the roadblock of ignorance.

2

The Wrong Concept of Deaconship

The Deaconship Traditional Ignorance: A problem in the church.

To be ignorant of truth or that which is true is not the worst thing. Traditional ignorance is worse than the fact of not just knowing. Traditional ignorance is falsehoods which are believed to be true or accepted as truth. When misinformation becomes enshrined in function and practice you have "traditional ignorance". As it relates to the deaconship and the church in general, we have a lot of misconceptions which have come to us from the past decades. Traditional ignorance is dividing and splitting many churches today. False concepts of the work have been passed down from on church generation to another. Let us consider a few misconceptions which plague the peace of many of our churches. If we are to get on with the work of the church and deaconship in particular, we need to dispel some of the myths and presumptions and we need to stay with the Bible.

The work of the church must be ordered by the clear teaching and commands of God's word. What individuals or groups think we should not form the word? What individuals or groups think, should not form the policy and practice of the church, neither the work of the policy and practice of the church, neither the work of the officers nor the auxiliaries. The church is the body of Christ. It is his to build, order, and command. He has said to us that the scriptures are sufficient in both directing missions, and methods of the church. Some deacons see themselves as supervisors of the pastor. Some have already written the concept of deacon's superiority in their constitution and or by-laws. At no time is the deacon the supervisor of the pastor. If we want to honor the teachings of the scriptures we must both pastor and deacon reject this supervisory concept of the deaconship. As we have previously stated "it is not reason" to see the appointee at the same rank as the appointer. Those who see deacons, as the watch dogs, so to speak of the church and supervisors of the pastor, in substance expect people to allow and accept this absurdity. No knowledgeable Christian deacon desires this bossy role. Even the pastor who has the right view of his office will lead God's people with love and compassion. The rule of love is not harsh. Love rules with kindness. The pastors are the overseers of the churches.

It is the place of the pastors who is Christ's under shepherd to council all that the church is not personal property. We are all stewards of the grace and mercy of God. Peter wrote to the elders (preachers or pastors) saying, "The elders which are among you I exhort, who am also an elder and a witness of the suffering of Christ and also a partaker of the glory that shall be revealed: Feed the flock of God which is among you, taking the oversight thereof not by constraint, but willing not for filthy lucre, but of a ready mind; Neither as being lords over God's heritage, but being ensamples to the flock." (1 Peter 5:1-3) Many brethren if this counsel of humility is given to the "Kingdom Key Men" whose office it is to oversee the congregation surely deacons who are ministerial staff men assistance of the pastors must be humble servant ready to follow the man of God as follow Christ.

The Crown Deacon: Another Misconception

Another misconception which some deacons have of them is this idea of being a "Crown Deacon". These so called crown deacons, see themselves as having some mythical right to the office of deacon. Once a deacon not necessarily always saved," this is true and is taught by scripture in a number of places. Passages such as (John 6:37) "All that Father giveth to me that cometh to me I will in no wise be cast out." Also in John 10:27-28, said, "My sheep hear my voice and I know them and they follow me: I give unto them eternal life; they shall never perish neither shall any man pluck them out of my hand." There is no scriptural proof nor is there any reason for us to believe "once a deacon always a deacon." Through a deacon may serve for life it is not automatic nor should it be.

There are many situations or circumstances that may arise which would make it advisable for one to discontinue his service as a deacon. In the New Testament both the apostles and church were in agreement as to who would serve. It should be so now. Deacons should serve at the pleasure of the pastor and the church. The pastor and church should agree as did the apostles and the church concerning who serve, who continues to serve, and who need arises is removed for service.

Never entertain this idea of being a "Crowned Deacon". Always remember the humble spirit of Jesus Christ. Jesus is the master pattern for all Christian workers, as it relates to attitude and spirit. Anyone who emphasizes that they are a "Crowned deacon" may have false concept of the deaconship. When one hears the word "Crown" one thinks of kingly authority. One who has a great personal merit above others? This whole idea regarding their being crowned may come from the misconception about the meaning of the deacon's ordination. There are no magic powers in the ordination service. These services inform the public that the pastor and church are setting men apart to this specific word whom they judge acceptable to the deaconship. The deacon's ordination is not a crown, but rather a token of office of service.

There should be no Masonic like rank among deacons. All deacons are brethren of equal rank. The "crowned deacon" concept is suspect because the use of "crowned' in the context of the deaconship suggest a proud heart. Humble service not pride should be the deacon's watchword. We should heed the scriptural warning to steer clear of pride. "Only by pride cometh contention; but with the well advised is wisdom." (See Proverbs 13:10) Yes, out of a heart of pride comes an argumentative spirit. People with quiet humble spirits are not the sources of contention. People with quiet humble spirits are not the sources of contention as strife. Deacons as other Christians should remember, Pride goeth before destruction and a haughty spirit before a fall. Better it is to be of a humble spirit with the lowly that to divide the spoil with proud." (See Proverbs 16:18-19)

The Deacon a Servant Leader

Serving at the tables of the church and working closely with the pastors deacons will be considered and honored as leaders. Yet, the deacons should remember that no Christian leader is worthy of the name accept it be prefixed with the word servant. Deacons are servant leaders or leading servants. Remember, even Christ was among us as one that served. "For whether is greater, he that sitteth at meat or he that serveth? Is not he that sitteth at meat? But, I am among you as he that serves." (See Luke 22:27) As the scripture said, "the servant is not greater that his Lord." The right call that comes to the Christian worker is the call to Christ likeness, "come unto me all ye labor and are heavy laden, and I will give you rest. Take my yoke upon you and learn of me; for I am meek and lowly in heart: ye shall find rest unto you souls." (See Matthew 11:28-29) if the deacon wants inner peace and rest it is found in working in the spirit of Christ. Christ likeness is the charge of every believer. "Let this mind be in you who was also in Christ Jesus: Who being in the form of God, thought it not robbery to be equal with God: but likeness of men" (See Philippians 2:5-7). Remember, Satan can handle and get a good grip on pride, but humility slips from his hand. Remember, also that it is the meek that shall inherit the earth.

They of a humble spirit shall be blessed with

the abiding presence of the almighty. "For thus saith the high and lofty One that inhabits eternity, whose name is Holy; I dwell in the high and holy place with him also that is of a contrite and humble spirit to revive the heart of the contrite ones". (Isaiah 57:15)Whenever God is there is both peace and power. A humble is the posture of power. A humble spirit is the posture of power. If you want to have power with God and power for God, let your spirit be won by humility. God inhabit the humble spirit. It is a sanctuary for his presence. Take your eyes off the world. The deacon work closes with the pastor, help him as much as you can, but in everything you do, do it as unto the Lord. Let your service be as it was acceptable offering unto the Lord. (See Ephesians 6:7-8)

THE CHURCH IS SELF GOVERNING

Ministration is defined in Webster's New Collegiate Dictionary as, "The act or process of ministering. Ministering, serving, hence ministration is the process or act of serving by whatever is the established method for a given kind of service. The deacon is the ministrant of the tables. He is the one who serves the tables or one who serves at the tables. Let no one confuse the word "ministration" with the word administration. Administration is the act or process of administrating. This is the performance of executive duties. Administration is management. One who administers is who supervises the execution and the conduct of the office. When Luke in Acts refers to the daily ministration he was talking about the process of the distribution of the church charities. "There arose a murmuring of the Grecians against the Hebrews because their widows were neglected in the daily ministration". The daily ministration of reference dealt with "serving tables" this was the giving out of gifts of benevolence. This was the business that brought the deaconship into existence. They were not set aside to "administer" the business of the church. Peter and the others appointed (deacons) over "this business" (serving of the church charities. The apostles had set the policy. We see this in their setting of the qualifications of the ministrants. (See Acts 6:3) The apostle did not have the time to be ministrants in every area over which they were administrators. In modern times, the deacon duties have been expanded to include the reception of all offerings given to the church conforms to the original idea of serving the tables.

However, "administration" of all these funds what some all taking care of the temporal affairs of the church, the concept is contrary to both the letter and the spirit of the letter found in Acts 6:1-4. The error is viewing ministration to be administration and viewing "this business" (which was ministration of the charities) to be the control of all financial matters of the church, hence, many think that their duty is to administer the temporal affairs of the church. The pastor is the administrator. Deacons are "ministrants" serving under the appointment of the pastor. J Alfred Smith said, "the duty of the deacons is to uphold the pastor's arms'. They do this by assuming the duties of distributing the charities. They must look to the administrator for the policy of distribution and if the pastor charges the deacon to set the policy of distribution, and if the pastor charges the deacon to set the policy for distribution. Policy making is limited to how the charities are administered.

The Power of the Church

As for the temporal affairs of the church, the church under Christ is in control of its own affairs temporal and otherwise. Jesus said tell it to the church. The New Testament church is a self-governing church. The pastor leads and feeds the deacons are the table ministrants. The church makes its own policies based on New Testament directives. The assembly will decide who will lead. The church assembly selects the deacons and turns them over to the leader for their appointment. The church under the pastor's leadership decides its own affairs and policies. The church has the last word. Jesus said when it comes to the final decision, "tell it unto the church". Preliminary, decisions may be made by others, but the final decisions belong to the church. (Colossian 1:18) He decides the policy decisions and this is the function of the head. What The head decides is reflected in the action of the body. Leaders may have their input which is their function, but Christ acts through his body; He is in the midst. (Matthew 18:17, 18 & 20) Study these passages which deal with the self-governing church.

Christ invested power in His body. We too often forget the great connection and interaction between the head and the body. This power is receiving, disciplining, and excluding its members is vested in any officers of the church. Only the church posses this power and as we have seen in

Matthew, Christ himself gave the church power to receive, discipline, and exclude its members. For an example of exclusion and restoration the prerogative of the body, see 1 Corinthians 5:1-5, 2 Corinthians 11:4-5, Romans 16:17, and 2 Thessalonians 3:6.

The Church has Power to Elect Its Own Officers

An example of the church election of its own officers is in Acts 1:15-26 and Acts 5:1-5; elections of delegate are shown in 1Corinthians 16:3; the election of Bishops, Elders, and pastors are found in Acts 14:23.Paul and Barnabas ordained elders in every city which were "chosen" by the churches (chosen, meant by vote of the uplifted hands). The church has power to decide all other matters not determined by scripture (see 1 Corinthians 14:40.) Please notice that the apostle directed their letters to the churches not to officers, or judicatories. There are no letters to call official boards or any group who could compare with a board of directors. Boards of directors are for secular companies. They are out of place in the church. Boards, committees, and officers are servants to and of the church. The church is governed by its members and lead by the pastor which is elected, and served by its deacon's board or committee should substitute the body. Boards, committee etc... carry out the will and order of the church not the reverse.

3

THE DEACON ON DUTY

The assistant to the pastor according to the Bible

The office of the deaconship has come down to us through nearly two thousand years of history. It has proved to be a permanent office in the church. The office has endured through changing times because there continue to exist in the church a role, and work for special helpers, of the gospel ministry. Some people feel today that the office of deacon has out lived its usefulness. This is not so. The New Testament church contains the patterns and directives for the church in all times. The times may change but, principles and pattern remained the same. There is still a need and even more so for godly men to enter the service of the deaconship. The pastor still needs to give himself to prayer and the study of the word. The deacon is the helper and assistant to the pastor. The deacon's major is not setting, but serving. He is not just someone with a little, but should be toiler in helping to advance the cause of Christ. There is joy and great reward for those who are workmen in the church. What are the specific duties of deacons in the modern Christian church? The nature of the deaconship has not changed. As you know, "deacon" means servant. This is an all-purpose worker. Whatever, his assignment the deacon's work should be some task that lightens the pastor's burden.

The Deacon Has Duty at the Table of the Poor

Today when people in the church and community contact the church for help, most of these calls come to the contact the church for help most of these calls come first to the minister. Through many of these calls come first to the attention to the pastor, they should be referred to the deacons. Administering benevolence to the

45

needy is the primary work of the deacons. Hence, the needs for honesty, the Spirit and wisdom are without exception. In fact, the pastor and deacons should inform the membership that when someone requires the help of the church, they should not contact the pastor, but rather the deacons. The members should be notified that if they contact the pastor, the pastor will be referring their request to the deacons for their determination. The deacons may well feel the need to confer, for council with the pastor for his advice in some cases, or just to keep him informed about the work being performed by the deacons. However, there is no need to burden the pastor about every simple case presented to the deacon staff.

The pastor and deacons may find it useful to draw up some basic guidelines for the administering of the poor fund. This can help to guide and aid the deacons in their decision making. Let the deacons remember that the church in the New Testament had no relatives who could assume that responsibility. Notice how the apostles Paul instructs pastor Timothy concerning guidelines for administering the charities of the church. Paul writes to Timothy because it was the pastor's responsibility to instruct the deacons and appoint them to their work. "Honor widows that are widows indeed. But, if any widows have children, or nephews, let them learn first to show piety at home, and to requite their parents: for that is good and acceptable before God." (1Timothy 5:3-4) The church cannot take care of everybody's needs. So there needs to be an understanding among the deacon staff what kind of needs should be given priority. Let able relatives help their own children. The limited resources of the church should go to help first of all "Widows Indeed" learn from first Timothy 5:3-16, some considerations that will enhance the poor or benevolent fund use. Study those verses and heed the teaching found there. Even when addressing needs other that the widows apply to all cases the principles of the most than the widows apply to all cases of the principles of the needy.

Standing at the tables of the poor, let the deacon stand there and serve, there informed about the principle of the needy and truly needy. A few people both in and out of the church will misuses the funds if they are allowed. Today, people with drug problems, alcohol problems or problems managing their affairs, will seek out ease-

"gifts horses" so to speak. The deacon and church should help where they can, but they should do so after some investigation or assurance that there is a genuine need. Let the deacons keep a good record of their work. This is advisable so that reports to the pastor and or to the church may be made when necessary. The deacon should keep a record of names of people helped, amounts, and dates. You need not report name in the deacon's report to the church; respecting the confidence of the people receiving help. Yet, let the deacons keep this factual information in their records. Some people make repeated request, and records on past cases can be helpful to the staff to make equitable decisions in the future. Let the deacon beware that in a few ceases some go from church-only, and last thief. Deacons must be compassionate, but also wise.

The deacons should be ready to inform the pastor and or the church about any special benevolent needs that may arise, but only if the needs cannot be met in the usual way. At the table of the poor the deacon can be an angel of mercy. Cautious to those who serve at this table do not presume to act as if the benevolent fund is your personal property. Some have used the funds to win points with certain people. Let us take-heed how we serve. In any case rewards for will come from God. The Lord has the record of our service. Pray to bless the cause and the Christ through your service at this table of mercy.

The Deacon at the Table of the Church

The deacons standing at the table of the church have a great opportunity for service. If the deacon standing at the table of the poor and he stands at the table of mercy, he's standing at the table of the church, stands at the table of service. The deaconship is no place for a man who doesn't have time, or take time to regularly attend worship. You cannot fulfill the purpose an aims of the deaconship at home.

Those passages in the book of Hebrew which encourage church attendance, certainly applied to deacons. Faithful attendance, certainly apply to the deacons. "Not forsaking the assembling of yourselves together as the manner of some is; but exhorting one another: and so much the more, as ye see the day approaching." (Hebrews 10:25) Not forsaking the assembly is an admonition, which goes out to all believers and members of the local church. However, the not forsaking should be underlined double where the deacons are concerned. This is also true for all persons with leadership responsibility. You must be at the table. Do not be an absentee deacon. Do not just be faithful in presence, but also in duty and service.

The Duty at the Table of the Church

Faithfully standing at the tables of the church the deacon working with other brethren can be a living letter of faith and faithfulness. Someone seeing you at the post of duty will be encouraged to stand and labor at their post of duty. Stand and serve at the table of the church. Stand there first as a faithful member. Stand there to give faithfully out of what the Lord have given you. Witness to Jesus by your words of sound doctrine, but first be the Lord's witness by your actions.

Faithfully standing at the table of the church giving cheerfully is the example. Remember the scripture teaches that God loves a cheerful giver. (see 11 Corinthians 9:7) If you really know that God is faithful and will keep his word, you can be a cheerful giver. Those of us who have genuine experience with God know that he'll do just what he said. You, who know God, know that you can lay down and get up on his word. The deacon who stands at the table of the church must have faith in God's word. Like the pastor, the deacon must be a faith practitioner. How and what we give reflects how and what we believe.

Show through your giving that you trust God to provide all your needs. Before you ask others to give, you give. Give faithfully, liberally, and cheerfully, knowing and believing the scripture that teach, "And God is able to make all grace abound toward you; that ye, always having all sufficiency in all things, may abound to every good work" (11 Corinthians 9:8). The deacon must be the one who can witness that the Lord will provide. Faithfulness in giving, and honesty in service will enable the deacon to earn that good degree of Godly honor, which is praise to them that use their office well. So then, the first duty of the deacons at the table of the church is not to receive the offerings of others, but rather to give his offering.

Faithfully, and cheerfully giving is the way to give, and tithes and offerings, is what to give. Let not the deacon come to the table not knowing what God requires. The deacon should understand that there is one and only on system given and approved by God to support the work of the church. The only system is tithes and offerings. (See Genesis 14:18-20; 28:20-22; Leviticus 27:30-33; Malachi 3:8-12) In both Testaments of the Bible, tithes and offerings is that one way God has sanctioned and ordered. God has not ordered the church body to sale anything for its maintenance and support. It is not out of line for individual church members to sale their possessions and property to help meet the needs, and ministries of the church. The church must not order or encourage individual members to sale their property. Let the members of the local church come by this decision on their own, like as did believers in the New Testament church. (see Act 4:32-37) In these verses in Acts, notice voluntary giving, "Neither said any of them that ought of the things which he possessed was his own; but they had all things common." (Verse 32) "...For as many as were possessors of lands or houses sold them, and brought the prices of things that were sold, and laid them down at the apostles' feet."

Notice the persons who possessed various properties sold what was theirs and brought the money to the church, but the church did not order them to do this. The apostle did not tell them to do this. The selling was the decision of the possessors. The church was involved in the receiving, not the selling. Please brother deacon come to the table of the church with the correct knowledge of God's way of supporting his church and his cause. No man stands at the table of the church and serve with wisdom that does not first possess adequate knowledge about the Bible's way of supporting the church. If wisdom is the correct use of knowledge then gaining correct knowledge is the first step toward wisdom. A deacon must be honest, full of the Holy Spirit, but he must also be a man of wisdom. Knowledge is the raw material from which wisdom is made. The shoemaker must first have the raw material before he can fashion his shoes. The car maker must have the metal before he can be a wise man in his craft. The deacon will come to the second table of duty with wisdom when he acquires the necessary knowledge about gifts, and attitudes which are well pleasing in the sight of God. Just ay gift that people give is not acceptable with the Lord. The giver should come to God's house to give what the Lord requires of his people. God is King, with a kingdom. Kings and governments have state tax requirement of the people subject to particular rules of the given kingdom.

No citizen obeying the laws of the kingdom of their servitude comes to the tax collector with the same amount which they themselves have determined. They rather come with the prescribed amount levied by our government, or tax assessors. Just like, our state and federal tax is levied by our secular government, so also the kingdom of heaven has levied a tax, and prescribed a way of giving to maintain and advance its cause in the world. Jesus did not spend long sermons or dissertations on tithing in the New Testament because the people of his day understood tithes & offerings were what God required of his peoples. The Jews knew and accepted, at least in principle. The Jews knew and accepted, at least in principle that the first tenth was the basic standard. It was the minimum gift required, (see Leviticus 27:30-33 and Proverbs 3:9, 10 "Bring the first tenth to the house of God." (See Malachi 3:10.) The tenth was the minimum; an offering was giving above the tithes. Notice, (one) tithes and (two) offerings. So you see you have not given an offering until you give the gift first required which is the tithe.

Let the deacons come to the table of the church with this knowledge that he may act with wisdom, aiding others to do the same. Before we conclude our study of the preparations deacons must have to effectively work at this second table let us understand clearly that God's way of supporting his house is not slightly altered by the New Testament. The New Testament magnifies God's way.

Giving As the Lord Has Blessed You

How many times have we heard a deacon standing at the table of the church or a minister from the pulpit saying, "it is time for the offering. We would like for you to give as the Lord has blessed you." This is a good saying. However, it has been spoken so many times without the true sense being given. It has become a signal for people to give whatever they want to give. Some people want to give as little they can without being embarrassed. It has been my experience that when someone says that, people ought to give as the Lord has blessed them, take this as a cue to give a dollar. Unless there is someone at the table who has understanding concerning the origin of the saying it will continue to be the cue for people to give little or nothing. To give as the Lord has blessed, or prospered you is a very good measuring rod by which to measure our giving. Now, help the people to think about to think about what it is that is being said.

Notice, for one to give underlines the tithe, and offerings concept. To give as the Lord has prospered all the same, at the same time. One should give "as" meaning according "to how" they assess God's giving to them and by that assessment measure their gifts to his cause. Both our tithes and our offering should be measured in the spirit of God's giving to us. Giving according to liability is the principle that should be kept in mind at all the tables of duty. Encourage people to think before giving. Let us think of God's goodness towards us. How do I value God's gift to me. Our gifts to the church should reflect God's goodness to us. Giving, "as God hath prospered" is the language that Paul used in encouraging the church at Corinth to give to poor saints. This language was used in concerning the tables of the church especially where offerings other than the tithe were being received. However, at the table of the church the deacon should stress the duty of the tithe first. Tithes are the gift of duty, because it is what God commanded us to do.

"Giving as God has prospered you" is also, as we have said proportional giving, is similar to the tithe. The difference being the in tithing the first tenth is claimed by God, "it is holy to the Lord." Give God that which is God's. This says that there is an offering of duty, the tithe. There is also the free will offering of various kings which is an offering of opportunity. Though the Lord requires free offering from his people, he does not set the amount of the free will offering. Hence, if he did so it would not be a free will offering. The free will offering will is left up to the worshipper's determination. An example of free will offering is seen in Paul's second letter to the church at Corinth. "Every man according as he purposeth in his heart, so let him give; not grudgingly, or of necessity; for God loveth a cheerful giver." (See II Corinthians 9:7) This particular reference deals with an offering of the "will", free will, not tithe or offering of necessity. Love prompts the believer to give beyond the requirements of law, and command. The giving "as" a man purposeth in his heart is not a substitute for the tithe, but is a love gift not to be as Paul said given grudgingly or out of necessity. The free will offering whether for benevolent, missions, or special projects are gifts of opportunity because for love of Christ they are given. Free will special projects are gifts of opportunity for the giver to bless others, the cause of Christ and themselves. Paul said much about the gifts of love.

"This is to say, he which soweth sparingly; and which he soweth bountifully shall reap also bountifully." (II Corinthians 9:6) (See also Proverbs 19:17; Ecclesiastes 11:1; Luke 6:38) When you have read the above mention passages you will see that giving to godly causes are opportunities for service, and blessings. God remembers the giver. He who blesses the cause of God will be blessed by God. There is a law of blessing which automatically comes to those who give from the heart cheerfully, and bountifully. Paul said this kind of giving is like sowing and reaping. He that sows reaps. He that sows sparingly will reap sparingly. He that sows bountifully reaps also bountifully. As the law of nature, so the law of spiritual giving, the sower reaps. As the sower reaps by the law of divine promise, so, also is the bountiful sower. Bountiful sowing is liberal giving. Bountiful "plenty" will be the receipt of them who give to Godly causes. Let the deacon study and learn what the Bible said about giving. The gospel of Jesus Christ concerns itself with God's gifts to us. God gave us his precious Son, his only begotten. This too was the gift of love. How great is the love of God to give so much to us, and this he did before we became his friends.

While we were yet enemies Christ died for us. Yes, the gospel of Jesus Christ is all about giving. The apostle James said, "Every good and perfect gift comes down from God." (James 1:17) God is a giver. Jesus Christ is a giver. Some people major in receiving, but Jesus bid us following him. With Jesus, giving was first, and because of his giving our Lord received the world as his inheritance. So, also will we receive and inherit the earth through our giving in the service of God. God promised to bless the gift of obedience. Those who through obedience would bring the tithe, and offering to his house, that there might be supplies in his house, he would open for them the window of heaven and pour them out a blessing. Great is the blessing received even to know that you have done God's Will! Great is the bounty of peace and joy which we receive serving and giving at the table of the church.

The Table of the Pastor

"Do ye not know that they which minister about holy things live of the things of the temple? And they which wait at the altar are partakers with the altar? Even so hath the Lord ordained that they which preach the gospel should live of the gospel?" (1 Corinthians 9:13-14) The deacon has the opportunity to serve God in a unique way as he stand at the table of the pastor. The table of the pastor is that place where the church comes to meet the financial needs of the pastor. Giving at the table of the poor is giving the gifts of mercy and compassion

Giving at the tables of the church is giving gifts of duty and love. Giving at the table of the pastor requires the same spirit necessary at the other tables. In giving to the support of the pastor, there is the area of duty, area of love, area of mercy, and compassion. Standing at the table of the pastor all skills you have acquired at the other tables may be and should be employed at this third table. Let us examine these three areas concerning the deacon's duty at the tables of the pastor.

The duty of the church to the pastor

When we say that there are three tables in the church the pastor's table being the third table we only refer to the obligation of the church to financially support its pastor. The Bible teaches in both Testaments this duty of the duty of the people of God toward the man of God. Being pastor to my brothers is a full time work. It is the Lord's work, but it is working in every sense of s the word. "And in the same house remain, eating and drinking of such things as they give: for the laborer is worthy of his hire.

Go not from house to house. (St. Luke 10:7) Yes, the minister of the gospel is a laborer. In the passages in Luke, our Lord's statement concerning the laborer being worthy of his hire was in reference to provision which Christ provided for the preachers on their evangelist, and or missionary travels. However, we learn that the preacher who is under specific assignment from the Lord who is serving the spiritual needs of the people is to be counted a laborer, worthy of his hire. If evangelist and missionary preachers are worthy of his hire certainly pastors who toil with a local congregation day after day and night after night are worthy of their hire also. Pastors have very defined and specific duties to perform on a continuous bases. Hence, Paul wrote concerning pastors. "Let the elder that rule well be counted worthy of double honor, especially they who labor in the world and doctrine." For the scripture said, Thou shalt not muzzle the ox that treadth out the corn. And, the laborer then it is right and the duty of those whom he serves to compensate him for full time service. Knowing what the scripture say about   pastors   being   worthy   laborers.

Deacons should be leaders in helping the church to adequately compensate the pastor. Too, often when it comes to blessing the pastor financially we stop at the word "we can't pay him (pastor) for the message of service he gives. We understand the great immeasurable value of the gospel and the service of the gospel preacher. Yet, to say "we can't pay him" what it's worth. We need not dwell on what we cannot do, but rather on the things that we can do with God leading and helping us. We can if will adequately take good care of our pastors who labor in the word and doctrine. Let us remember how the man of God admonished believers to let a Christ-like mind be in us. "I can do all things through Christ who strengthen me. (Philippians 4:13) At the table of the pastor, deacon should not swell on what we cannot do. God does not require his people to do things they cannot do. But, he does want them to do what they can and should. The Lord requires his people to take care of the material needs of those who minister about spiritual things. Remembesr, how Paul wrote, "Do ye not know that they which minister about holy things live of the things of the temple? And they which wait at the altar? Even so hath the lord ordained that they which preach the gospel should live of the gospel?" (1 Corinthians 9:13-14) So, that duty is laid upon the church to take care of him who takes care of them.

This duty also charge the church and it's leaders not only to do certain things for the pastor's care, but also the scripture orders the church not to withhold or hinder the provision which are rightfully assigned and marked our for his third table. "Who goeth a warfare anytime at this own charges? Who planted a vineyard and eateth not of the fruit thereof for who feedeth a flock, and eateth not of the milk of the flock? Say these things as a man? Or saith not the law the same, for it is written in the laws of Moses, thou shalt not muzzle the mouth of the ox that treadeth out the corn. Doth God take care for oxen? Or said he it altogether for our sakes? For our sakes, no doubt, this is written: that he that plow should in hope;..." (1 Corinthians 9:7-10) In these matters the pastor needs someone to help assure that his needs are met. Then he shall be better able to look out for the welfare of the church body.

A drowning man can hardly cast the lifeline to others. We must come to the table of the pastor seeing and being faithful to our duty. The scriptures lay duty upon us, but love has moved us to duty with compassion and understanding. They who preach and labor so hard to life us to new heights in the Lord surely they are worthy of our efforts to hold them up. Here at this third table the deacons in the church of today may look to the past for inspiration. Moses had help and helpers. Moses could not have achieved many of the wonders and great victories without help from faithful men who could not have achieved many of the wonders and great victories without help from faithful men who stood to support him. Remember, the battle which the children of Israel fought in this battle when the arms of Moses were lift up they prevailed over their enemies, but when his arms grew weary and were lowered in the sight of Israel they got the worst of the battle and the enemy prevailed over them some alert men say what was happening. They went to the sides of Moses and stood there with him upholding his arms. Hence causing Israel to defeat their enemies and prevail in the battle. (See Exodus 17:9:4)

There has always been a place and ministry for those who assist the Lord's anointed leader. Deacons can and should uphold the hands of the pastor. By doing so, the church will prevail over the enemy and the cause of the kingdom of God will be advanced. It was so in the Old Testament time. It was so In the New Testament times. Remember, how Luke wrote in Acts after the selection of the seven, who stood to serve the tables. "And the word of God increased and the number of disciples multiplied in Jerusalem greatly, and great companies of the priest were obedient to the faith." (Acts 6:7) The good work of your church will increase when deacons serve the purpose of the selection. The deacon serving at this third table can and should be an agent of progress as well as an angel of compassion.

Be sure the pastor is properly compensated and that adequate provisions be made by the church and its vast operational programs for him and his family. Come to this table of service with both wisdom and love. It is a post of duty, but love will transform it into a post of opportunity and joy. Love for God and his servant, the pastor, will compel men who are honest, full of the Holy Spirit, and wisdom to serve, ever praying at this table, as well as others. All things with are done by prayer, and nothing without prayer. Let each officer stand at this third table of duty to the honor and praise of God.

THE DEACON AND WORSHIP

Deacons in the Missionary Baptist churches all over America have assisted pastors in the capacity of devotional leaders. What a privilege to serve and an opportunity to witness the reality of the faith which is in Jesus Christ. Some of the most precious memories I have about worship have to deal with spirit filled deacons in worship. As they conducted devotional services at worship time the power came. I was there when it came. I was there when they prayed, moaned, and sung. I know the privilege and power of prayer, come from where deacons were calling on God. Never, will I forget them, in their humble services as devotional leaders. If I pause to think, I can hear them, in their praying now. Greater St. Luke Baptist Church in Jackson Tennessee I remember men of prayer and men of power. As a young minister, I was there with them on Wednesday night in prayer meeting. Unity and they joy of the lord were there. I was glad when the time came to rehearse the devotional hymns. We sang the long meters, the short meters,, the common meters, behind each hymn somebody would pray. There were many new voices, but the way had been well laid. God blessed those men and the thousands like them the nation over, many whom I have not seen nor heard.

Yet, I know something of the value of the number of deacons or luminaries in the universe of my personal experience. Deacons can and should be lights and live wires today. The deacons worship tools are the Bible, a hymnbook, and a prayerful spirit. All good deacons are not in the past. There are many serving well now, and hopefully there will be many more in the future, Deacons as leaders of devotion in worship can witness as they work. This will occur when their work is a witness as they work. These will occur when their work is a witness. When God moves upon the deacon in worship as he reads, sings, and prays, can, will, and should positively impact someone's life. By praying and practicing hymn with the deacons, I saw that God met them at their post of duty and there pour upon them his Spirit empowering them for this and there upon them His Spirit empowers them for this and other service. Kneeling at the footstool of mercy one will not only be a conductor of power, but a receiver of power. Born again, prayerful deacons are often power situations for God. God dwelling in the prayer service at the beginning of the worship will remain with that church service throughout the worship. When humble men pray, God is always present. Praying deacons; "what an aid to preachers and preaching." It is useful and desired by men of God who themselves, come in the power of the Spirit to bring a word from the Lord. Deacons please do not take devotion and its influence lightly. It all began at the throne of grace.

A praying church is a powerful church. Remember what happened on Pentecost power and wonders of Pentecost begin with a prayer meeting. "These all continued with on accord in prayer and supplication, with the women and

Mary the mother of Jesus, and with the brethren." (Acts 1:14) Power will always come when Christians unite in prayer. Those that come to the throne of Grace with faith will go away with the blessing. Bow before God knowing that he sees all of your cares. Bow while looking and listening for his footsteps. Bow while believing and knowing that he is able to lift you? Bow knowing that God is worthy to be praised. God is worthy of our entire honor because he is the source of all. Bow that you in his strength might rise to praise him and go forth to magnify him among the people. There are many deacons today maybe not as many as there could be who give themselves in the worship service. Come let us worship the Lord, he has promised to meet us. Remember how he said, "again I say unto you, that if two of you shall agree on earth as touching anything that they shall ask, it shall be done for them of my Father, which is in heaven. For where two or three are gathered together in my name, there am I in the midst of them." (St. Matthew 18:19-20) Deacons should major as leaders in worship. They should know the book of Psalms. I thank God for deacons, who major in worship.

DEACONS ON DUTY BAPTISMAL SERVICE

Equity and balanced participated from the brother I am very much desired. A duty roster should be established which utilizes the entire staff. You will need to assign someone to prepare the baptismal pool for use. Certain brothers should be assigned to assist the pastor with the actual baptism. Someone may be needed to go into the water with the pastor. Help in the water with the pastor. Help in the water may be determined by size of the pool, the number and/or size of the candidates. Be alert, see when, and where help is needed. There will need to be at least two deacons assisting candidates in and out of the pool. It will also be need to cover the pool after baptizing is over dependant on the kind of pool you have. There will also be a need to clear the area for other use. The pastor may need the assistance of the brethren in leading the baptismal devotional service. Have appropriate scripture ready if asked to read. Be ready with song and prayer. Do your specific assignment and be ready to assist in others if asked.

The deacons will need to coordinate their efforts with the deaconess in assisting the male

70

candidates. For teenage boys years upward the deacon should be prepared to council concerning what they will need in terms of garments for baptism. Deacons should encourage and direct these young people to orientation classes and/or Sunday school class. Remember to mail out rotation roster. All deacons should share and participate in this duty. The deaconess will assist and help the female candidates. They will council and prepare them for this important service, however, let the deacon stand ready to help the deaconess in any help they may require.

DEACONS ON DUTY AT THE TABLE OF THE LORD

There is a table that deacons today are called to serve. This is the table of the Lord. The deacons are responsible for preparing this table for service. Deacons should see to it that deaconess, mother or ministers' wives have the necessary items and article for the supper. Brothers, be sure there is an adequate supply of wine, glasses, serving trays, etc. The deaconess should prepare the bread and clean the linen and be sure that white gloves are ready for use. The deaconess will actually prepare the table for use, but it is the deacons who will carry the table in or stand at the assisting the pastor with serving the bread and wine.

The serving at the table should be organized, so that each deacon will know his assigned duty. Roster assignment and prior communications before the supper will eliminate a need to talk at the table. Assisting the pastor, each man in his place, will help the good order of things and the solemnity of the service. Always dress as becoming Christian men at all times. For the Lord's Supper, if possible wear black suits with white shirts. Coordinated dress helps to convey a spirit of unity and oneness among the brothers. Remember, the deacon staff is a fellowship of men with common purpose. Let unity be expressed in what we say, in how we act, and in what we wear. Let all the brothers come to this, the table of the Lord prayerfully with our minds on the sacrifice of our Lord Jesus Christ at Calvary.

THE DEACON ON DUTY IN VISITING NEEDY MEMBERS

Caring for widows and other needy members may require more than an occasional gift. Sick or disable members may need aid at home or just the fellowship of other believers. Often there are many deacons, but there is but one pastor. Assisting the pastor in the area of visitation can really be a big plus for everyone. Sharing and bearing the burning of the work is so needed today. There are some pastors and churches that operate a ward system.

In the ward system, each deacon is given a portion of the membership to serve. He may collect their offering when they are unable to attend or communicate some message of information about coming events, projects, etc. However, whether or not your church employs the ward system deaconess' should coordinate a visitation roster. Care and love should be, beyond the walls of the sanctuary.

Make a list of the windows and current needy and sick members make some assignments. Some people may want to volunteer for certain assignments, but be sure that all deacons and deaconess share this important work. Remember how Jesus taught us concerning our Christian duty (see St. Matthew 25:34-36). Let it not be said of you and your deacon staff (see verse 41-45). Show real compassion for the needy brother or sister. Being some joy and peace put your love in action, keep records of your visitations. Where appropriate, pray and read with the sick and the shut-in. See passages in the back of the book. Let all us respond to the needs of the needy.

4

The Deacon and His Family

The family of a Deacon is holy unto the Lord...

The deacon has a unique office in the church. He must be a flexible man. On one hand he must have humility and follow the lead of the under Sheppard whom God has placed in the church. On the other had he must be a leader of his wife and children. The deacon must be a leader and a follower. This is to say the deacons should be examples of good fellowship. Hence, they are to lead followers.

Those who serve under the pastor and out of the office of the pastor, by virtue of their place of service bare leadership responsibilities. There is a great need in the modern Christian church for missionary Baptist deacons to be the servant leaders which the scriptures orders and challenges leading example of fellowship in the church, they must learn and strive to be the leaders of their own homes. The scriptures require deacons to be "not just" a leader in the home, but the leader of the home. The deacons' leadership of his family is not a service and responsibility given him by virtue of the deaconship. This call to lead his family comes from the highest office in the universe.

Men, of whom a few are deacons, are changed of God to be leaders of their own home. You should supply leadership for you own family. In Paul's charge to deacons in 1st Timothy, we find this counsel, "Let the deacons be the husbands of one wife, ruling their children, and their own houses as well" (1Timothy 3:12). If the deacon is the leader (ruler) of his own house then his obedience to the will of God is evidence by his conduct at home. God has appointed men to be rulers (head) of their wives (see Genesis 3:16; 1Corinthians 11:3, Ephesians 5:22-23, also see 1Peter 3:1-7). (The above mentioned passage, take the time and study them). Like Jesus Christ the head of the church, the deacons' rule at home ought to be the rule of love and sacrifice. Men must rule, but they must also love. They must lead their families as if their homes were to be homes after God's design, but they must give themselves for their wives and children. Love does not rule with an iron hand. The rule of love is the rule of gentleness. The rule of love is the rule of righteousness. The rule of love understands. The rule of love is the rule of peace. Christ is our example of a ruler, under God's directions.

He feeds the church. The deacon who honors Christ must take responsibility of family leadership and feeds his family. He must nourish his wife and children. Christ gave himself for the church, giving his life for it. Husband hence, deacons must give themselves sacrificially for his family. If situations demand, he must deny himself, to the benefit and welfare of his family. As the man in the home the deacon has a charge for the Lord also, to labor and earn a living to provide for his own family. The deacon must take charge and have good control of his children. You can be a better leader in the church when you are the leader of your home. Let the deacon remember that you can lead better when you live better. A wife or children do not mind following a husband or a father who demonstrates his love for them and his godly attitude toward them. Honor God in your home. God made the man first and the man should put God first also. The man of the home should lead the family in the worship of God. He must go before them as he, and they go after Christ. The deacon looking at the individual needs of each family member must learn to keep them before the Lord in prayer. Prayer makes things better. Prayer makes people better. You should be the prayer leader at home not only praying for your family, but praying with your family. Godly examples go a long way.

Take time to be a father and a husband. Be unselfish in your giving to your loved ones. Love generates compassion. Remember, God will see your labor and he will remember you. He will supply your every need. As you care for your family, God will care for you. Remember, whatever you lack as you look to God he will teach you he will guide you. He will make you sufficient for your task both in the home and in the church. Lean on God, look to him for strength. We also need him to illuminates our pathway. God must be your light, don't be wise in your own eyes there are taps, trails, and troubles, which we cannot see well enough to manage. We must ever call to mind the word that says, "Trust in the Lord with all thine heart and learn not unto thine own understanding. In all thy ways acknowledge him, and he shall direct thy paths." (See Proverbs 2: 4&6.) Therefore, my brothers when you face the task of family leadership humble yourself before God. First commit yourself to him, and then commit them whom have given you to his care and protection. God is well able to supply theirs and you every need.

5

A Deacon Is a Growing Disciple

The deacon should grow as other believers in Jesus Christ. He should grow both in the knowledge and grace of our Lord Jesus Christ. He should study to learn from both his experience of God's grace and God's word. The Bible is written word of God. We know that Jesus is the word of God which liveth and abideth forever, and the scriptures are they that testify of him (St. John 5:39). The scriptures are true and cannot be broken, meaning it cannot be altered (See John

10:35; also II Timothy 3:16). Therefore we have a charge to keep. Our charge is to study "Study to show thyself approved unto God, a workman that needeth not be ashamed, rightly dividing the word of truth" (II Timothy 2:15). The scriptures are the word of truth. The following passage should be studied individually or collectively by the deacon staff. Let us begin at the beginning.

THE DEACON A GROWING DISCIPLE: GOD AS A WORKMAN WITH PRIORITIES GENESIS 1:1-2; 4

(A) The first days of work; the creation of light. Genesis 1:1-5, Remember God is a great example for laborers. He did the first things first. Light was created first because it was needed first. Light would be a needed instrument in the study of creation. In your study, please consider the importance of light in the natural world and in the spiritual world. Remember that God is light (I John 1:5) God created light because the world needed light. Darkness everywhere, the writer said, "Darkness was upon the face of the deep."

(B) THE SON OF LIGHT FOR OUR SPIRITUAL DARKNESS

Spiritually the world was in the dark after the fall of man. God seeing our need penetrated the darkness of sin with the living of the light of his own presence. "Verily, verily, I say unto you, He that entereth not by the door into the sheepfold, but climbth up some other, the same is a thief and a robber. But he that entereth in by the door is the shepherd of the sheep. To him the porter openeth; and the sheep hear his voice: and he calleth his own sheep by name, and leadeth them out. And when he putteth forth his own sheep, he goeth before them, and the sheep follow him: for they know not the voice of strangers.

This is the parable spake Jesus unto them. Then said Jesus unto them again, Verily, Verily I say unto you, I am the door of the sheep. All that came before me are thieves and robbers: but the sheep did not hear them. I am the door: by me if any man enters in, he shall be saved, and shall go in and out, and find pasture. The theif cometh not, but for a steal, and to kill, and to destroy; I come that they may have light, and that they may have life, and that they might have it more abundantly. (St. John 10:1-10) Truth is light and truth should rank first with us. All our subsequent labor will be void if we do not labor in truth, and because of truth. It is never safe to follow the blind, if we are to be leader in the service of God who is truth, and light, how shall we honor his purpose except we be lovers of truth. We should always remember that without truth there is no real freedom. Only truth makes one free. (See St. John 8:32, 36)

What can we learn from this study? (1) We learn that light was the first thing God created. This makes light the priority creation and it being necessary for subsequent creation. Light therefore is primary to all that God does. (2) We learn that God's word is light, and God's word is truth. This is true because God himself is light and God himself is truth. (3) We learned that God came to us in Jesus Christ. He being the light of world declared his deity. Jesus was God, living light shining in the midst of us.

The second day God created firmament (atmosphere). In the firmament he placed the gases hydrogen, oxygen, nitrogen, etc.... All of these elements and in combination of elements would be weather elements. The second day God made the upper part of his ecological system for light to operate. The power of light already presents to operate upon the elements which were made on the second day.

Third day God made the bottom half of his ecological system which would house his creations. The earth is a kind house wherein God would place what he made. On the second day he built his atmosphere, and having in place the atmospheric gas he made the living things which those gases would support. He put first things first. He creates plants bearing seed, each after its own kind. The third day God created seas, and land, and vegetation. "And God said, Let the waters under the heaven be gathered together unto one place, and let the dry land appear; and it was so. And God called the dry land Earth, and the gathering together of the waters called the Sea; and God saw that it was good.

And God said, Let the Earth bring forth grass, the herb yielding seed, and the fruit tree yielding fruit after his kind, whose seed is in itself upon the earth; and it was. And the Earth brought forth grass, an herb yielding after its kind

, and the yielding fruit, whose seed was in itself after his kind: and God saw that it was good. And the evening and the morning were the third day.

LESSON THREE: GOD AN ORDERLY WORKMAN

The fourth day God created heavenly bodies Sun, Moon, and Stars. They were for signs and seasons, for days and years. Go created the instruments of time. The movements of the heavenly bodies gave us our seasons. "And God said Let there be lights in the firmament of the heaven to give light upon the earth; and it was. And God made two great lights, and the greater light to rule the day, and the lesser light to rule the night; He made the stars also" (see Genesis 1:14-16). Also study the passages in Ecclesiastes 3:1-15 and also St. John 9:4.

What can we learn from this study? There are doubtless a number of things. However, let us point out a few lessons. (1) We learn from the fourth day's creation that God is orderly in all that he does. We also remember the scripture that say, "Let everything be done decent and in order." (2) Also from the creation of seasons, we learn that God is in control of time. Hence, we know him as Lord of the harvest. (3) We learn that God meet timely needs of man. Each season brings supply for human needs. (4) We learn that life is seasonal. Things come in their order and in their time.

LESSON FOUR: GOD AN EXEMPLIARY WORKMAN

The fifth day God created animal life of the sea and air. The earth in the preceding days was prepared for living inhabitants. The fifth day, God created living things in the sea and the air. Even upon earth itself, the God of time is timely. God's wisdom is reflected in his action. The creatures of water and air come to the stage of existence at the proper time. "And God said, let the water bring forth abundantly the moving creature that hath life, and fowl may fly above the earth in the open firmament of heaven. And God created great whales, and every living creature that moveth, which the waters brought forth abundantly, after their kind, and every fowl after his kind; and God saw that it was good. And God blessed them, saying, Be fruitful and multiply, and fill the waters in the seas, and let the fowl multiply in the earth. And the evening and the morning were the fifth day (Genesis 1:20-23.)

What did we learn from this fifth day of labor? (1) We learn that God is the life giver (2) His wisdom is so complete and sufficient that he accomplished his aims. He finishes his work prepared days before. We can learn to follow through. Some people are good at beginning but they fail to complete their work. We must not only start we must carry out work to completion. We must learn to do as the poet who wrote, "I am going through." Yes, I am going through, I started with Jesus, and I am going through. God is the supreme pattern for determination laborers.

He creates light, air, water, and vegetation, then, he brings those creatures to the stage that will make use of all of his preparation. (3) We also learn that God is not limited in wisdom or in power the fifth day reflects wisdom at work. His wisdom worked. What marvelous wisdom, so many different living things. If we view the creatures as machines, we see that they all work. His fish swimming, his birds flying, his lions roaring and etc... and reproduces their own kind omniscience and omnipotence were twin laborers. When we consider the animal kingdom of the sea and air, we see God to the processor of unlimited wisdom and power.

LESSON FIVE: GOD OUR PURPOSEFUL WORKMAN

On the sixth day of creation he continued to create living creatures. The highest forms of living creatures are created on the sixth day. Cattle, creeping things, and beast are all created on the sixth day. These also produced after their kind. "And God said, Let the earth bring forth the living creature after his kind, and everything that creepeth upon the earth after his kind; and God saw that it was good." (Gen. 1:24-25) Five times in verse twenty, 24 and 25 we see the use of the words, after their kind. All land the land creatures produce a seed exactly like themselves. This producing after their kind argues against evolution. Animals don't evolve, they produce their own kind. Let God be praised. Apes gave birth to other apes. Apes do not give birth to man nor men like creatures. They don't evolve into some other kind. We learn that dumb animals produce their own kind; hence, there is no reason and order in everything that he did.

THE MAKING OF MAN

The crowning work of creation was the creation of man. Genesis 1:26-2:7 look for the answers to these questions.

1. What is man?
2. Whose man?
3. What is man's purpose for being?
4. How do we know that man is not a product of natural evolution?

Give your answer to these questions. Think about these questions, read, and pray and then give your answers.

In the list of the other lessons try to follow the pattern set in lesson one, two, and three. Write down in your own words what you've learned from the studies. Do each list after each session.

OTHER LESSONS TO STUDY

GOD'S ORIGINAL COPY OF THE FAMILY:

Read and study Genesis 2 verse 8-25 of chapter two. This chapter may be divided in to three parts or lessons.

LESSON SIX MAN'S FIRST HOME Genesis 2: 8-17

THE GARDEN OF WONDER Genesis 2 vs. 10-14, EDEN A WATERED GARDEN

Get a map and see if you can locate these rivers, see if you can get the general area of the location of Eden. There are noted rivers there. Learn the names of four rivers.

GOD COMMANDS HIS COMMANDER (Genesis 15)

(a) The Command of God's law. God commanded that man not to eat of the tree of good and evil, at the same time permitting him to eat of every other tree. Man is given the responsibility of choice. It is a life or death choice.

(b) A divine deliberation and promise, "and the Lord God said, it is not good that man should be alone, I will make him a help meet for him." Vs. 18

(c) God grants the man royal authority verse 19-20

(d) The making of a woman, her purpose, and place. Verses 21-25
List in your own words what you have learned from a study of chapter two, lesson six.

How do you think this knowledge will help? Take time to do this assignment. Compare your notes with other brothers, and discuss the relevance of the true you have learned. This is seen in her purpose for being made; "she" is made for him (a companion for him) "she was his own rib." She was brought to him. She was brought to him. She was named by him. Adam authority over Eve before sin entered is also seen in God allowing him to name her "sex"; "she shall be called woman." Verse 23, Adam also gave her, her personal name "Eve", seen in verse 20, Chapter three of Genesis. Also before sin entered Adam's authority over Eve is seen in his position in paradise. He is dresser, and keeper of the garden. The male authority over the woman is also seen in his reception of the law. God commanded the man. (See Genesis 1:17) He calls the man to account first to answer he was God's appointed leader of the family. After sin entered the world this did not change man's responsibility as leader of the family. The proof may be seen in Genesis 3:16, God said to the woman, I will greatly multiply thy sorrow and thy conception in sorrow thou shalt bring forth children; and thy desire shall be to thy husband, and he shall rule over thee" There is no change in leadership responsibility because in man's penalty, he is charged to be the breadwinner. (See verse 17-19). Their spiritual status changed. Proof of this is seen in their expulsion from their Study Genesis Chapter three: the fall of man.

Study this chapter with a view of answering the questions. What changed after sin and fall what did not change? List everything you can find that changed after the fall, also list things separately that did not change? How do you account for the thing that did not change? Answer this question in your own words. After you have studied the lesson and given your answers, discuss each other's findings. You may want to form separate discussion groups. One group focusing on the things that sin changed the other groups on things that did not change as a result of human transgression. After you have discussed the lesson for about a half hour, the group will come together and compare notes. Is there basic agreements, list the disagreements if any, use biblical proofs to decide any differences. Ask the pastor to help bring light on the subject if desirable, or needed.

Let me give you one example each, of things that changed after sin and also things that did not change.) After man sinned, his authority over woman did not change. Notice before sin entered the world, God gave the male authority over the woman. Garden paradise see verses 22-24, third chapter of Genesis. There were often things that changed, and still others that did not change. Genesis 4:1-17, Examine both worshippers and their offerings. Examine what makes one acceptable, and the other unacceptable. Study Genesis verses 1-17. Write the answer to the question, and list other things learned from the study. How may we use these lessons?

HELPFUL SCRIPTURES FOR THE DEACON ON DUTY

1. When visiting the sick, share with them one of the following passages.

*Psalm 39:12-13, Hear my prayer, O lord, and give ear unto my cry; hold not thy peace at my tears, for I am a stranger with thee, and a sojourner, as all my fathers were.

*Psalm 103:1-5 Bless the Lord, O my soul, and all that is within me bless his holy name. Bless the Lord, O my soul, and forget not all his benefits: who forgiveth all thine iniquities who healeth all thy diseases, who redeemeth thy life from destruction;

who crowneth thee with love and kindness and tender mercies, who satisfieth thy mouth with good things, so that thy youth is renewed like the eagles? See also: Psalm 25:16-18, Psalm 43:2-5, Psalm 46:1-2 & 10 vs. (emphasize 1&2) Psalm 23 and Isaiah 45:22

2. **When falsely accused:**

>   *Psalm 27:12-14, Deliver me not over unto the will of mine enemies; for false witness are risen up against me, and such as breathe out cruelty. I had fainted, unless I had believed to see the goodness of the Lord in the land of the living. Wait on the Lord, be of good courage, and he shall strengthen thine heart; wait, I say, on the Lord.

>   *St. Mathew 5:8-9, Blessed are the pure in heart; for they shall see God. Bless are the peacemakers; for they shall be called the children of God.

3. **When in need of guidance:**

A growing disciple

*Psalm 25:1-5, Unto thee, O Lord, do I lift up my soul. O my God, I trust in thee; let me not be ashamed, let not mine enemies triumph over me. Yea let not that wait on thee be ashamed: Let them be ashamed which transgress without cause. Show me thy ways, O Lord; teach me thy paths. Lead me in thy truth, and teach me: for thou art the God of my salvation: on thee do I wait all the day.

4. **When one is recovering from illness:**

*Psalm 27:10-11, I will extol thee, O Lord; for thou hast lifted me up, and hast not made foes to rejoice over me. O Lord, thou hast brought up my soul from the grave: thou hast kept me alive that I should not go should not go down to the pit. Sing unto the Lord, O, ye saints of his, and give thanks at the remembrance of his holiness. For his anger endureth but a moment; in his favor is life: weeping may endure for a night, but joy cometh in the morning. And in my prosperity I said, I shall never be moved. Lord, by thy favor thou hast made my mountain to stand strong: thou didst hide thy face, and I was troubled. (See also Psalm 40:1-5 and Psalm 91: 1-7)

5. **When one is in need of forgiveness:**
   *Psalm 25:6-7, Remember, O Lord, thy tender mercies and they loving kindness; for they have been ever of old. Remember not the sins of my youth, or my transgressions: according to thy mercy remember thou me for thy goodness' sake, O Lord.

   *Psalm 39:7-11, And now, Lord, what wait I for? My hope is in thee. Deliver me from all my transgressions: make me not the reproach of the foolish. I was dumb; I opened not my mouth; because thou didst it. Remove thy stroke away from me; I am consumed by the blow of thine hand. When thou with rebukes dost correct man for iniquity, thou makest his beauty to consume away like a moth; surely ever man is vanity.

A growing disciple

6. The blessedness of forgiveness:

*Psalm 32:1-5, Blessed is he whose transgression is forgiveness, whose sin is covered. Blessed is the man unto whom the Lord imputeth not iniquity, and in whose spirit there is no guile. When I kept silence, my bones wax old through my roaring all the day long.

*Isaiah 44:22, I have blotted out, as a thick cloud, thy transgression, and as a cloud, thy sins: return unto me; for I have redeemed thee.

7. When one has been delivered from trouble:
*Psalm 34:1-9
I will bless the Lord at all times; his praise shall continually be in my mouth. My soul shall make her boast in the Lord: the humble shall hear thereof, and be glad. O, magnify the Lord with me, and let us exalt his name together. I sought the Lord, and he heard me, and delivered me from all my fears. They looked unto him, and were

lightened; and their faces were not ashamed. This poor man cried, and the Lord heard him, and saved him out of all his troubles. The angel of the Lord encampeth round about them that fear, and delivereth them. O taste and see that the Lord is good; blessed is the man that trusted in him. O, fear the Lord, ye his saints; for there is no want to that fear him.

See also Psalm 92:1-5 & Psalm 150

8. **When the wicked have much and you have little:**

    *Psalm 37:16-24, A little that a righteous man hath is better that the riches of many wicked. For the arms of the wicked shall be broken; but the Lord upholdeth the righteous. The Lord knoweth the days of the upright; and their inheritance shall be forever. They shall not be ashamed in the evil time, and in the days of famine they shall be satisfied. But the wicked shall perish, and the enemies of the Lord shall be as the fat of lambs; they shall consume away. The wicked borroweth and payeth not again; but the righteous sheweth mercy, and giveth. For such as be blessed of him shall inherit the earth and they that be cursed of him shall be cut off. The steps of a good man are ordered by the Lord; and he deligheth in his way. Though he fall; he shall not be utterly cast down; for the Lord upholdeth him with his hand. (See psalm 49:12-20)

9. **When enemies plot against the faithful:**
   *Psalm 35:1-3 (see verses 4-23), plead my cause, O Lord, with them that strive with me: fight against them that fight against me. Take hold of the shield and buckler and stand up for mine help. Draw out also the spear and stop the way against them that persecute me: say unto my soul I am they salvation.
   *Psalm 38:19-22, but mine enemies are lively, and they are strong: and that render evil for good are mine adversaries because I follow the thing that is good. (Also see Isaiah 41:10-12)

10. **When one give to anger:**
    *Psalm 37:7-15, Rest in the Lord, and wait patiently for him: fret not thyself because of him who prospered in his way because of

the man who bringth wicked devices to pass. Cease from anger and forsake wrath; fret not thyself in any wise to do evil. Deuteronomy 32:35, Isaiah 63:4, Psalm 94:1, Romans 12:19, Proverbs 6:34, Hebrews 10:30, Proverbs 16:32, Ecclesiastes 7:9

11. **When in danger or trouble:**
   *Psalm 23
   *Psalm 27
   *Psalm 31

In thee, O Lord, do I put my trust; let me never be ashamed: deliver me in thy righteous. Bow down thine ear to me; deliver me speedily; be thou my strong rock, for my house of defense to save me.

*Isaiah 49:1-2, Listen, O Lord, do I put my trust; let me never me in thy righteousness. Bow down thine ear to me, deliver me speedily; be thou my strong rock, for a house of defense to save me.

*Isaiah 49:1-2 see also Isaiah 45:2, Listen, O isles, unto me and harken, ye people from far. The Lord called me from the womb;

from the womb; from the bowels of my
mother hath he made mention of my name.
And he hath made my mouth like a sharp
sword, in the shadow of his hands hath he
hid me, and made me a polished shaft; in
his quiver hath he hid me.

*Isaiah 54:17

12. When encouraging one to trust in God:

*Psalm 37:1-11, Fret not thyself of evil
doers, neither by thou envious against the
workers of iniquity. For they shall soon be
cut down like the grass and wither as the
green herb. Trust in the Lord and do good;
so shalt thou dwell in the land and verily
thou shalt be fed.

*Psalm 57:1-7, be merciful unto me, O God,
be merciful unto me; for my soul trusteth in
thee; yea, in the shadow of thy things I will
make my refuge, until these calamities be
over past. I will cry unto the God that
performeth   all   things   for   me....
*Psalm 56:1-9, Be merciful unto me, O God,
for man would swallow me up; for they are

many that fight against me, O though most High. What time I am afraid, I will trust in thee... See also 60:10-12

13. When encouraging one to righteousness:

Mark the perfect man, and behold the up right; for the end of that man is peace. But the transgressors shall be destroyed together; the end of the wicked shall be cut off. But the salvation of the righteous is of the Lord; he is their strength in the time of trouble...

*Isaiah 51:7, Hearken unto me, ye that know righteousness, the people in whose heart is my law; fear ye not the reproach of men, neither be ye afraid of their revealing. "For the moth shall eat them up like a garment, and the worm shall eat them like wool; but my righteousness shall be forever and my salvation from generation to generation..."

*Isaiah 52:1-3, Awake, awake; put on thy strength, O Zion, put on thy beautiful garments, O Jerusalem, the holy city; for henceforth, there shall no more come into thee the uncircumcised and the unclean. Shake thyself for the dust; arise and sit down, O Jerusalem, loose thyself from the bands of thy neck, O captive daughter of Zion…. See also Isaiah 51:10-12; 56:2; 33:1-5

14. When the faithful person is in need of God's help:

*Psalm 40:8-17, I delight to do thy will, O my God; yea, thy law is within my heart. I have preached righteousness in the great congregation; lo, I have not refrained my lips, O Lord, thou knowest.

*Isaiah 54:14-1, In righteous shalt thou be established; thou shalt be far from oppression; for thou shalt not fear, and from terror; for it shall not come near thee… Now weapon that is formed against thee shall prosper, and every tongue that shall rise against thee in judgment thou shalt condemn. This is the heritage of the servants of the Lord, and their righteousness is of me, saith the Lord....

15. When the tongue needs control:

*Psalm 39:1, I said, I will take heed to my ways, that I sin not with my tongue; I will keep my mouth with a bridle, while the wicked is before.

*James 3:2-10, for in many things we offend all. If any man offend not in word, the same is a perfect man, and able also to bridle the whole body. Behold, we put bits in the horses' mouths, that they may obey us; and we turn about their whole body...

*Proverbs 18:6-8, a fool's lips enter into contention, and his mouth calleth for strokes. A fool's mouth is his destruction, and his lips are the snare of soul...

(Liars love to listen to lies: see Proverbs 17:4)

16. When the charitable needs help:

*Psalm 41:1, blessed is he that considereth the poor; the Lord will deliver him in the time of trouble. The Lord will preserve him, and keep him alive; and he shall be blessed upon the earth, and thou wilt not deliver him unto the will of his enemies...

17. When forsaken or betrayed:

*Psalm 41:7-13, all that hate me whisper together against me; against me do they devise my hurt. An evil disease, say they, cleaveth fast unto him, and now that he lieth he shall rise up on more. Yea, mine own familiar friend, in up his heel also against me... See also Psalm 27:9-10

19. When encouraging one to pray:

*Psalm 55:17, Evening and morning, and at noon, will I pray, and cry aloud: and he shall hear my voice.

Deacons are growing disciples

*Psalm 64: 1 Hear my voice, O God, in my prayer: preserve my life from fear of the enemy.

*St. Mathew 26:41, Watch and pray, that ye enter not into temptation: the spirit indeed is willing, but the flesh is weak.

*I Peter 3:12 For the eyes of the Lord are over the righteous, and his ears are open unto their prayers but the face of the Lord is against them that do evil... Isaiah 45:22; St. Luke 18:1: Luke 11:1, Isaiah 56:7; James 5:3; I Thessalonians 5:17; 3:10

20. When one is in need of strength:

*Isaiah 46:4, And even to your old age I am he; and even to hoar hairs will I carry you: I have made, and I will bear; even I will carry and deliver you...

*Isaiah 40:10, Behold, the Lord God will come with strong hand, and his arm shall rule for him: behold, his reward is with him, and his work before him...

A growing disciple

*Isaiah 41:40, Fear thou not: for I am with thee: be not dismayed: for I am thy God: I will strengthen thee: yea I will uphold thee with the right hand of my righteousness.... See also Isaiah 40:29-31; Psalm 28:6-9

21. When there is bereavement:

*St. John 14:1, Let not your heart be troubled: ye believe in God, believe also in me.

*St. John 11:25-26, Jesus said unto her. I am the resurrection, and the life: he that believeth in me, though he was dead, yet shall he live: And whosoever liveth and believeth in me shall never die. Believeth thou this? Read Psalm 23; Psalm 46:1-3; 6-11

22. When encouraging one to study the Bible:

*II Timothy 2:15, Study to show thyself approved unto God, a workman that need not to be ashamed, rightly dividing the word of truth...

Deacons are growing disciples

Read also Timothy 3:16; Isaiah 40:7-8, St. Mathew 24:35; St. John 5:39, 6:63

23. Devotional Readings

Psalm 19:1-14, Psalm 31:1-3, Isaiah 60:1-4, Psalm 84:1-4, Psalm 100, Psalm 105:1-5, Psalm 127, Psalm 150, Psalm 116:1-7, Psalm 119:57-64

THINGS TO REMEMBER

1. **The cause of Jesus Christ comes first**
   St. Mathew 10:37 also St. Luke 14:26-27; "I am Alpha and Omega, the beginning and the ending, saith the Lord, which is, and which was, and which is to come, the almighty Revelation 1:8

2. **God has the power, if you have the faith**
   St. Mark 9:23 also 11:22-24

3. **Pray and forgive**
   St. Mark 11:24-26

4. **Pray one for another**
   St. James 5:16

5. **Remember Lots wife**
   St. Luke 17:32-33

6. **Be a good listener**
   Isaiah 50:5 and St. Mathew 11

7. **Work and be diligent**
   Proverbs 6: 6; Proverbs 18:9

8. **Be timely**

QUESTION FOR EXAMINATION OF DEACONS

1. **What person, if any, who you have been regenerated and born again?**
   <u>ANS</u>. I know that I have been born again of the spirit of God.

2. **How do you know you have been converted, and now a new creature in Christ?** <u>ANS.</u> Because my love for Christ, his cause and his church.

3. **What is a church according to the teachings of the New Testament?**
   <u>ANS</u>. Based on the teachings of the

4.   Deacons are growing disciples

5.   New Testament; a church is a band or group of baptized believers in Christ, who have united by a covenant to carry out the commands and ordinances given by our Lord Jesus Christ.

6.   How many ordinances are there in the Baptist church? And what are they? (give names)

ANS. Two ordinances in the Baptist church. Baptism & the Lord's Supper.

7.   How many true God's are there?

ANS. There is only one true and living God. He is revealed to us as Father, Son, and Holy Spirit. Each with distinct personal attributes, but without division of nature essence or being.

8.   By what mean are sinners saved, or what is the way of salvation and what scriptures could you give as proof of your answer?

ANS. Salvation is wholly of Grace.

9. **Based on the teaching of the New Testament, what is the Christian Sabbath Day of worship?**
10. **What are duties of Deacons in the church?**
11. **What is regeneration?**
12. **How many scriptural officers are there in the church?**
13. **Should a pastor clear his program and plans for the church with the deacons before carrying them into church?**